Ezra
A Mountain Lion

by
Bonnie Highsmith Taylor

Perfection Learning®

Dedication
For Steven Bulger

About the Author
Bonnie Highsmith Taylor is a native Oregonian. She loves camping in the Oregon mountains and watching birds and other wildlife. Writing is Ms. Taylor's first love. But she also enjoys going to plays and concerts, collecting antique dolls, and listening to good music.

Ms. Taylor is the author of several Animal Adventures books, including *Kip: A Sea Otter* and *Roscoe: A North American Moose.*

Book Design: Randy Messer
Cover Image: Corel
Image Credits: *Art Today* (images copyright www.arttoday.com) pp. 4, 7, 8, 9 (top), 14, 15, 16 (top), 17 (top), 19 (all), 20, 25, 26, 29; *Corel* pp. 5, 6, 9 (bottom), 10, 11, 12, 13, 16 (bottom), 17 (bottom), 18, 21, 22, 24, 27, 28, 30, 31, 32, 33, 34, 35, 36, 39, 41, 42, 45, 47, 48, 51, 53

Text © 2001 Perfection Learning® Corporation.
All rights reserved. No part of this book may be used or reproduced in any manner whatsoever without written permission from the publisher.
Printed in the United States of America. For information, contact Perfection Learning® Corporation, 1000 North Second Avenue,
P.O. Box 500, Logan, Iowa 51546-0500.
Tel: 1-800-831-4190 • Fax: 1-712-644-2392

Paperback ISBN 0-7891-5166-9
Cover Craft® ISBN 0-7807-9313-7

Contents

Chapter 1 6
Chapter 2 13
Chapter 3 21
Chapter 4 27
Chapter 5 39
Chapter 6 47

Chapter 1

It was early June. But it was still cold in the high mountains. That was where the young female mountain lion lived.

For several days, she had searched for a den. It had to be in a safe place. It had to be warm and dry. And it had to be a good place to give birth to her kittens.

Mountain lions usually have their young in caves. Sometimes caves cannot be found. Then the lions make dens in holes under uprooted trees.

Places that are hidden and out of the weather are good for dens. Old deserted buildings have become dens for mountain lions and other animals.

One mother mountain lion gave birth in an old boxcar. It had been part of a train that had rolled down a steep hill. For three years in a row, she returned to the boxcar to have her kittens.

The female searched on and on. She had to find a den soon.

Until a little over six months ago, the young female had stayed with her mother. Her two brothers had left when they were a year old.

The female was just over two years old. A little over three months ago, she had mated. This would be her first time to give birth.

The male would have no part in raising the kittens. As a matter of fact, he might even kill the kittens if he saw them.

The female lion grew hungry. She had not eaten since the day before. And then, she had only eaten a rabbit. She had been too busy looking for a den site.

But now, she must take time to hunt for food. She needed her strength to give birth.

At dusk, she killed a deer. She ate her fill. Then she covered the rest of the deer with leaves, sticks, and dirt. If she was still in the area tomorrow, she would eat some more.

The warm, fresh meat filled her stomach. She crawled into a thicket and slept.

Early the next morning, she returned to her kill and uncovered it. She ate as much as she could. At a nearby creek, she drank thirstily. Then she continued her search.

The mountain lion climbed higher toward a huge rock pile. She saw an opening in a rock wall. It was at the edge of a flat, grassy area. But it was surrounded by boulders.

The female crept toward it slowly. She raised her head high. She curled back her upper lip and sniffed the air. No scent came from the opening.

The mountain lion went inside. It was warm and dark. It was about eight feet deep and over six feet wide. The ground was dry and soft. It was a perfect place to give birth.

The female lion went outside again. She scratched the ground all around the area. She urinated on rocks and bushes. She was marking her territory. This was her home.

She was very tired now. She went back inside the cozy cave and fell asleep.

Chapter 2

About noon the next day, the female's labor began. She lay at the back of the dark cave.

She heard many sounds outside. Sounds of singing birds drifted in. Some were still building nests. Others were feeding newly hatched baby birds.

Frogs croaked. They were in a small pond at the foot of the rocky cliff.

The female lion trembled at the sound of howling wolves. But they were very far away.

She listened intently. Their howls became weaker and weaker. The wolves were probably way beyond the river. The lion relaxed some.

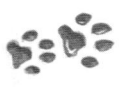

Between her labor pains, she napped lightly. The pains grew stronger.

Late in the day, Ezra was born. He weighed about one pound. He was ten inches long.

His blue eyes were tightly closed. His tiny ears were turned down and lay flat against his head. He was not a solid color as his mother was. His dark brown fur was covered with black spots. There were dark rings around his short tail. He was born with sharp claws.

His mother washed him with her rough tongue. Ezra squirmed and mewed.

He could not see or hear. But he could smell. His mother's scent was very strong to him. He would always know her smell.

Shortly after the female finished washing Ezra, her second kitten was born. It was a female. She looked exactly like Ezra. But she was a little smaller.

The mother cleaned the female kitten. She chewed the cords from the kittens' stomachs.

At last, the mewing kittens found their mother's nipples. They pawed against her stomach. They nursed hungrily. The female mountain lion was very tired. She purred loudly as her new babies nursed.

The kittens filled their stomachs. Then they fell into a sound sleep.

The female lion cleaned herself. She spent a lot of time washing and grooming herself as all cats do.

The lion finished her grooming. Then she went outside and ate some grass.

Once more, the female marked her territory. She urinated all around the area. She made deep scratches on fallen logs and trees.

After that, she went back into the cave. She sniffed her babies. Then she slept.

The following evening, the mother lion went hunting. She stayed close to her den.

The female sniffed the air as she walked. She smelled a deer before she saw it.

The deer was drinking water from the pond. The female cat lowered her body closer to the ground.

Silently, she crept toward the young doe. When she was 20 feet from the deer, the lion sprang.

The deer bolted. And the chase began. The mountain lion usually could run as fast as the deer—about 35 miles an hour. But she could only run this fast for a short distance. And now she was weak from giving birth.

Mountain lions' bodies are not built for speed. They try to sneak up on their prey. Then they spring through the air and land on top of the animal.

Sometimes lions wait on rocky ledges or in trees. As deer pass, the lions drop down on the deer.

The average mountain lion kills about 50 deer a year. This keeps deer populations under control. Often lions kill deer that are old and sick. They cannot outrun the lions. This is nature's way of thinning the herds and keeping them healthy.

Mountain lions prefer deer. But they will eat beavers, rabbits, hares, squirrels, muskrats, wild turkeys, and grouse. They also eat insects, frogs, and snakes.

Like most cats, lions eat grass. Sometimes mountain lions are very hungry, ill, or wounded. Then they will eat *carrion*, the flesh of dead animals. Mountain lions usually feed on wild game. But they have been known to kill livestock. There have been a few cases of humans being killed by mountain lions. But this is rare.

Hunting game is hard work. A predator is usually only successful half of the time.

This time, the female had to go to bed hungry. But Ezra and his sister filled their stomachs with warm milk. They were as full as possible when they fell asleep.

Their mother cleaned them as they slept. She licked the urine and feces from their bodies. This was how she kept the den clean. Her empty stomach rumbled. She curled around her two kittens and went to sleep.

Chapter 3

Ezra was two weeks old. His blue eyes were open. He could see his mother now.

He and his sister played. They tumbled about in the den. They made growling sounds as they wrestled.

Sometimes, their play got a little too wild. Then their mother would hold them down with a big paw.

Ezra hated that. He hated being washed too. But no matter how much he howled and struggled, he couldn't get away.

There are over 100 names used for the mountain lion. Its scientific name is *felis concolor*. *Felis* is Latin for "cat." *Concolor* means "one color." The lions are called *cougars, pumas, panthers,* and *catamounts.* There are many more Spanish and Native American names.

When early settlers first saw the *felis concolor*, they thought the animals were female African lions. Then they realized that none of them had manes. The settlers had never seen animals like them before.

Mountain lions are beautiful, large cats. They are the largest cats in the United States.

Mountain lions can be several different colors. They range from light tan and gray to reddish brown.

Grown males are about seven and a half feet long. They weigh between 150 and 175 pounds. Some are larger.

Females average about seven feet in length. They weigh between 100 and 125 pounds.

Mountain lions' heads seem too small for their bodies. The lions have long, sharp claws. Their claws can be pulled back when the lions don't need them.

Their tongues are very rough. The lions can lick meat right off the bones of their prey.

Mountain lions once roamed most of the United States. They were killed off in great numbers by early settlers.

Today, they can still be found in the western states and in some areas of Louisiana and Florida. The mountain lion is the state animal of Florida.

Mountain lions live in almost any kind of country or climate except the Arctic. They live in deserts and in high mountains. They like rocky areas best.

They use large boulders as look-out points. Perched on high cliffs, they can see long distances.

Mountain lions usually hunt at night. But if they are in areas far from towns and cities, they hunt any time. They are very secretive. So they are seldom seen by people.

Ezra was born far from towns. His mother had never seen a human. But one day, that all changed.

Chapter 4

The kittens' ears now stood up. They looked like their mother's ears. Every day, the kittens grew larger and stronger.

Their wrestling matches often got out of hand. Sometimes Ezra made his sister yowl loudly. Then his mother would pick him up by the scruff of his neck and move him away from his sister. Ezra hated that. He liked being the master in the scuffles.

Through the opening of the den, Ezra could see outside. Tree branches blew in the wind.

Once, he saw a small snake slither along the ground. He thought about pouncing on it. But it disappeared before he made up his mind.

Ezra was growing restless. He was tired of staying in the dark den. He was usually asleep when his mother left to go hunting.

Then one day, the female took her kittens outside. It was so exciting!

Ezra raised his head high. The breeze tickled his nose. It ruffled his fur. He liked the way the outdoors felt.

He cocked his head to one side. He heard a grouse beating its wings. What a strange sound. He moved closer to his mother. His sister started back to the cave opening.

The mother lion made a deep sound in her throat. She seemed to say, "Stay here. It's nothing to be afraid of."

The strange noise stopped. The female kitten came back.

Suddenly, a very large bird flew low overhead. The mother lion made a loud snarling sound. She even showed her teeth.

Ezra crouched a little. He had never heard his mother make such an angry sound.

Mountain lions make many different sounds. Each sound probably has a meaning.

When they're content, lions purr. They sound just like house cats. But they purr much, much louder.

Mountain lions also meow, hiss, spit, scream, growl, and grunt. They make one sound by whistling and fluttering their tongues. They sound like birds. This seems to be the sound they use to call one another.

The mother cat had snarled at an eagle. Eagles are a danger to baby animals. They can grab small animals in their long claws and carry them off to eat.

Ezra and his sister did not wander far from the den opening. Ezra saw a small plant moving back and forth in the breeze.

The plant looked like something fun to play with. He swatted at it with one paw. His sister joined in. They both swatted at the plant for a while.

Then they began to wrestle.

Soon the kittens were tired. Their mother took them inside the den. They nursed until their stomachs were full of warm sweet milk. Then the brother and sister curled up together and slept.

The mother mountain lion left the den to go hunting. She wandered a little farther than she usually did. She entered an open meadow.

Suddenly, she picked up a scent. It was a scent that was new to her. It was not the scent of a deer or a rabbit. Nor was it the scent of any other animal she knew.

Then she heard a sound. It was a loud clomping sound.

Then she heard another sound. It was a sound she had never heard in her life. It was the sound of human voices.

The female looked over her shoulder. Coming out of a wooded area were two men. They were on horseback.

The lion's heart jumped in her chest. She ran. She had never run so fast in her life. What were these creatures with the strange smell and sounds?

Suddenly, a shot rang out. It echoed against the mountains. At the same moment, a sharp pain pierced the lion's thigh. For a split second, her body jerked.

Then she heard loud human yells. She ran faster and faster.

The clomping hooves were like thunder. The lion ran into the woods at the edge of the meadow. She dodged trees as she ran. She crossed a stream.

The hunters rode after her. But the horses could not move as fast through the trees.

On and on the mountain lion ran. Her fear was stronger than the pain in her thigh. She had to get to her kittens.

At last, the female came to a steep, rocky hill. Over the pounding of her heart, she could still hear the horses. They were running. But they were farther away.

Another shot rang out. The bullet hit a boulder just ahead of her. Sparks flew!

The lion climbed over rocks. Higher and higher she went.

Blood ran down her leg. Her thigh throbbed. But still, she climbed on. Finally, she realized the sounds had nearly faded away.

From her spot on the high ridge, she could see the horses and riders. They were headed back across the meadow.

Luckily, they didn't have dogs with them. Dogs used for hunting mountain lions don't easily give up a chase. They would have tracked her by her scent and the blood that dripped from the wound.

Bounty was paid on mountain lions as early as 1500. By the mid-1970s, there was concern that the lions might become extinct. Many laws were changed regarding mountain lions.

Today, they are still hunted. The hunters are mostly cattle ranchers and *trophy hunters*, or people who hunt for sport.

In some places, laws have been passed recently making it illegal to hunt mountain lions with dogs.

The female lion lay on a flat boulder. She panted hard. She licked the blood from her fur. Her thigh burned and throbbed.

The wound was not deep. But it was painful. And it bled a lot.

Several hours later, she crawled into the den. She was sure that she had not been followed.

Her kittens were sleeping soundly. She licked the wound for a long time. Then she, too, fell asleep.

For the next few days, the female lion nursed her wound. She licked it with her long, rough tongue.

Once, she went to the creek and squatted down in the cold water. After several minutes, she got out. She shook herself dry. Then she licked the wound again.

Chapter 5

At six weeks, Ezra tasted his first meat. It was rabbit. The mother brought a small piece to the den. She dropped it on the ground. Then she lay down to groom herself.

Ezra approached the meat slowly. He smelled it. He licked the blood. He liked the taste. It was not as good as his mother's milk. But he did like it.

Then his sister walked toward the meat. At once, Ezra grabbed it and growled. The female kitten growled back. She made a lunge for the meat.

Both kittens tugged at the food. Each kitten swallowed a small bit of the rabbit.

At two months, the kittens were big enough to follow their mother about outside. Ezra weighed nearly ten pounds. His sister weighed about a pound less. Like most young animals, they spent much of their time playing.

The mother lion never again went back to the meadow where she had been shot. She took her kittens to open fields. But she tried to stay close to wooded areas. And most of the time, she waited until dark to take them out.

Ezra rambled along behind his mother. He listened to the night sounds. Owls hooted. Frogs croaked. Wind blew through the tops of tall trees.

There was one sound Ezra didn't like. He did not care for the sounds of howling wolves—even if they were a long way off.

Sometimes, the lion took her kittens on longer walks. Once in a while, they stopped and rested.

One night, the cats lay down under a tree for a brief rest. But Ezra was not tired.

Ezra wanted to play. When his mother's tail twitched, he pounced on it. She growled loudly.

Ezra knew she meant business. So he tried to play with his sister. She growled too. And she bit him!

Finally, Ezra lay down. He tried to sleep. But he was not sleepy. He rolled over a few times.

Then he found a pinecone. He lay on his back and held it between his paws. He chewed on it.

As he looked up, he saw something move in the pine tree. He watched, wide-eyed.

It moved again. It was coming down the pine tree. It crept lower and lower. Suddenly, it stopped on a low branch. It was only six feet from the ground. But it had spotted the cats. It froze.

Ezra got to his feet. He moved to the trunk of the tree. He looked straight up at the animal. The animal looked down at him. Ezra mewed. The animal grunted.

The mother lion heard the animal grunt. She got up and began walking away quickly. She called to her kittens.

Ezra didn't want to go. He wanted to watch the animal in the tree. Maybe it was something he could play with. Finally, he ran along to keep up with his mother and sister.

At last, the cats were out of sight. The porcupine came down from the tree and went on its way.

By the middle of September, the female stopped nursing the kittens. When Ezra tried to nurse, his mother would pull away and growl. Once she even cuffed him.

Sometimes a mother lion will let her kittens nurse a little longer. This depends on how much milk she has and whether hunting is good.

But Ezra began eating more and more meat. Soon, he forgot about nursing. He and his sister still fought over their food. But they both got their share.

Their mother had to hunt more often since the kittens were not nursing. And the kittens were not yet old enough to hunt.

One day, the mother lion was off hunting. Ezra was prowling around the edge of a pond. He caught a frog!

But Ezra was not able to hold on to it. The frog jumped away. And Ezra chased it. The frog was stunned and not able to jump far.

Twice, Ezra almost closed his jaws on it. But the frog always managed to leap away.

Finally, the frog gave a mighty jump and landed in the pond. Ezra also gave a mighty leap. And he landed in the pond.

Was he ever surprised! He had never been wet before. And he didn't like it at all!

The water was not deep. Ezra scrambled out. He shook himself as dry as he could. Then he licked himself and smoothed his fur.

Mountain lions can swim quite well. They have been known to swim across rivers to escape hunting dogs. But they are not fond of water.

Chapter 6

The first snow fell in the mountains. Songbirds had flown south. Bears had gone to sleep for the winter. Many other animals had denned up also.

Pikas lived in the rocks above the cats' den. They were well prepared for winter. Pikas are small animals that look much like guinea pigs. They live in colonies in rock piles.

Ezra had tried many times to catch the pikas. But they were too fast for him. And they had too many places to hide.

By the time Ezra was six months old, he weighed nearly 45 pounds. His sister was still a little smaller.

It was time for the young lions to begin hunting on their own. They were not ready to attack large animals like deer. That would be dangerous. Even full-grown mountain lions have been injured or killed by deer and elk.

Ezra had watched his mother hunt. He would know how when the time came.

Then one day, Ezra made his first kill! It was a snowshoe hare. It was hard work. The young lion zigged and zagged behind the hare for a long time. But finally, his strong jaws closed down on the hare's neck. It died instantly.

Ezra panted as he carried the hare to a spot at the edge of the meadow. He laid the hare down under the trees. The snow was not so deep there.

Using his sharp teeth, Ezra pulled the fur from the hare's neck. This was where he started his feast. How delicious the warm blood and meat tasted.

It was a large hare. Ezra could not eat all of it at once. He buried what was left in the snow. He covered the mound with dead leaves and sticks. Later, he would return to finish eating it.

Ezra was a very successful hunter. He caught birds, rabbits, and mice.

During the winter, the cat family hunted only in the daytime. It was warmer.

And now, deer were as active in the daytime as at night. The mother lion could show her kittens how to hunt them.

Ezra and his sister still spent much of their time playing. They chased each other in the snow. They wrestled. They leaped over fallen logs.

Sometimes, their mother joined in the fun. When Ezra and his sister attacked her, it was all she could do to handle them.

It was fun to clamp down on their mother's long tail. She pulled them through the snow as she tried to get loose.

The winter was long and cold. But the cat family had plenty to eat. The mother lion was a good hunter and killed at least one deer a week.

The kittens were able to catch many smaller animals. They never went hungry.

Though the winter was not too hard on the mountain lions, spring was welcome.

Songbirds began to make nests. Bears woke from their long sleep. By June, small animals were out of their burrows and dens. They frisked about in the new green grass.

The young lions had made it through their first year. They were both strong and healthy. They had a good place to live and hunt.

Some young lions leave their mothers when they are a year old. But most stay longer—usually about two years.

Ezra still lived with his family. But he often stayed away for days at a time.

As he roamed about, he marked the territory. He sprayed urine on logs, trees, and rocks.

Once, while roaming in a new area, he came face-to-face with an adult male mountain lion. Before the big lion had finished growling, Ezra was out of sight.

For two years, the young lions stayed with their mother. The female left first. She would mate soon. Then she would have her own family.

Ezra was much larger than his mother now. He weighed nearly 175 pounds. He was 32 inches high at the shoulder.

Ezra was a skilled hunter. He had no trouble bringing down a deer. Once, when he was all alone, he killed an elk.

The mother lion was ready to breed again. Several male lions came to the area. Ezra decided it was time for him to leave and find a territory of his own.

In a few months, his mother would have a new litter of kittens. They would be born in the same den where Ezra had been born.

Ezra would never see his siblings. And he would never see his mother again.

Over the years, Ezra would mate with several female mountain lions. He would father many kittens. But he would never know them.

Humans are about the only enemy mountain lions have. If Ezra was lucky and escaped hunters, he could live to be 15 to 20 years old.

For more information, contact

Mountain Lion Foundation
PO Box 1896
Sacramento, CA 95812
(916) 442-2666
MLF@mountainlion.org
www.mountainlion.org